BESIDE
Bethesda

JONI EARECKSON TADA

NAVPRESS®

A NavPress resource published in alliance
with Tyndale House Publishers, Inc.

NavPress is the publishing ministry of The Navigators, an international Christian organization and leader in personal spiritual development. NavPress is committed to helping people grow spiritually and enjoy lives of meaning and hope through personal and group resources that are biblically rooted, culturally relevant, and highly practical.

For more information, visit www.NavPress.com.

Copyright © 2014 by Joni Eareckson Tada. All rights reserved.

A NavPress resource published in alliance with Tyndale House Publishers, Inc.

NAVPRESS and the NAVPRESS logo are registered trademarks of NavPress, The Navigators. Absence of ® in connection with marks of NavPress or other parties does not indicate an absence of registration of those marks.

TYNDALE is a registered trademark of Tyndale House Publishers, Inc.

ISBN 978-1-61291-712-2

Cover design by Jennifer Ghionzoli

Cover frame copyright © Sergey Kandakov/Shutterstock. All rights reserved.

Cover photograph used courtesy of Zugr/Unsplash.

Published in association with the literary agency of Wolgemuth & Associates, Inc.

All Scripture quotations, unless otherwise indicated, are taken from the Holy Bible, *New International Version,*® *NIV.*® Copyright © 1973, 1978, 1984, 2011 by Biblica, Inc.® Used by permission of Zondervan. All rights reserved worldwide. www.zondervan.com.; Scripture quotations marked TLB are taken from *The Living Bible*, copyright © 1971 by Tyndale House Foundation. Used by permission of Tyndale House Publishers, Inc., Carol Stream, IL 60188. All rights reserved.; Scripture quotations marked NLT are taken from the Holy Bible, New Living Translation, copyright © 1996, 2004, 2007, 2013 by Tyndale House Foundation. (Some quotations may be from the NLT1, copyright © 1996.) Used by permission of Tyndale House Publishers, Inc., Carol Stream, Illinois 60188. All rights reserved.; Scripture quotations marked MSG are taken from *The Message* by Eugene Peterson, copyright © 1993, 1994, 1995, 1996, 2000, 2001, 2002. Used by permission of NavPress Publishing Group. All rights reserved.; Scripture verses marked PH are taken from *The New Testament in Modern English* by J. B. Phillips, © J. B. Phillips, 1958, 1959, 1960. All rights reserved.; Scripture quotations marked ESV are taken from *The Holy Bible*, English Standard Version® (ESV®), copyright © 2001 by Crossway, a publishing ministry of Good News Publishers. Used by permission. All rights reserved.; Scripture quotations marked NKJV are taken from the New King James Version.® Copyright © 1982 by Thomas Nelson, Inc. Used by permission. All rights reserved.

Library of Congress Cataloging-in-Publication Data

Tada, Joni Eareckson.

  Beside Bethesda / Joni Eareckson Tada.

    pages cm

  ISBN 978-1-61291-712-2

1. Sic—Religious life. 2. Sick—Prayers and devotions. 3. Spiritual healing—Prayers and devotions. 4. Spiritual healing—Christianity. I. Title.

  BV4910.T33 2014

  242'.2—dc23   2014017313

Printed in China

20	19	18	17	16	15	14
7	6	5	4	3	2	1

Dedication

For my pain-pal friends I've met by the pool of Bethesda.
With each devotional in this book, I pray for them. . . .

Gloria Blowers	Todd Lipe
Sam Britten	Bob Martinez
Steve Bundy	Brad Mattes
Heidi Clark	Steve Mays
Barbara Coleman	Nancy Meador
Michael Easley	Dolores Michaelson
Debbie Faculjak	Kristie Nanes
Deborah Fonseca	Kevin Natale
Jim French	James Rene
Ken Frenke	Theresa Schwartz
Lyn Futrell	Holly Strother
Randy Hart	Brad Stubblefield
Diana Hays	Rika Theron
Tim Ispas	Brittany Volpei
Don Krebs	John Williamson
Chris Leech	

These friends, like me, deal daily with pain.
Together we are discovering that grace always heals deeper.

*Now there is in Jerusalem near the Sheep Gate
a pool, which in Aramaic is called Bethesda and
which is surrounded by five covered colonnades.
Here a great number of disabled people used to
lie—the blind, the lame, the paralyzed. One who
was there had been an invalid for thirty-eight
years. When Jesus saw him lying there and learned
that he had been in this condition for a long
time, he asked him, "Do you want to get well?"*

*"Sir," the invalid replied, "I have no one to help me
into the pool when the water is stirred. While I am
trying to get in, someone else goes down ahead of me."*

*Then Jesus said to him, "Get up! Pick up
your mat and walk." At once the man was
cured; he picked up his mat and walked.*

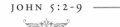

JOHN 5:2-9

Do Not Pass Me By

IF YOU SPEND ANY TIME at all with me, you will know that I love the old hymns. I love to hear them, and I love to sing them. But for me, it's something more than nostalgia or enjoying a particular style of music.

I don't just sing hymns because I want to.

I sing because I have to.

I remember darker days when I was first injured and in the hospital. I wanted so much to cry—and to just go on crying for the rest of my life. Instead, I would stifle the tears and comfort myself with one of the old hymns of the church:

Savior, Savior,
Hear my humble cry;
While on others Thou art calling,
Do not pass me by.

When I sang those words, or even hummed the melody softly to myself late at night in my hospital room, it always reminded me of the pool of Bethesda in John chapter 5. When friends visited me at the hospital, I often asked them to read that passage to me.

John speaks of one man who had been there, lying beside that pool, for thirty-eight years. The account goes on to say that "when Jesus saw him lying there and learned that he had been in this condition for a long time" (verse 6), He approached the disabled man and asked him a question.

I can't tell you how many nights I would picture myself there at the pool of Bethesda, on a blanket, perhaps lying next to the paralyzed man on his straw mat. In my mind's eye we would lie there, waiting. He would be waiting for an angel to stir up the waters. Then, somehow, he would inch himself over to the pool and slip into it for supernatural healing.

He was waiting for an angel . . . but I was waiting for Jesus.

I knew that the Son of God Himself would be coming, stepping out of the bright morning light, slipping under the shade of the colonnades and standing for a moment, looking out at the desperate, nearly hopeless little band of disabled men and women waiting at the water's edge.

In my fantasies, I would see Him pausing by the pool, His disciples puzzled by the delay and eager to keep moving toward the temple. And I would cry out to Him, not wanting Him to leave, not wanting Him to miss me, lying on that pavement in the shade of a pillar.

"Jesus! Oh, Jesus! Don't pass me by. Here I am! Heal me! Help me! Don't leave me here like this!"

And the truth was, though I couldn't see it at the time,

He had seen me all along. He had known me. He was aware of my fear, my sorrow, my despair, my longings, and my crushing need. He would not—did not—pass me by. He never has passed me by. And He never will, not in all eternity.

Jesus' ceaseless watch-care and compassion for us is no fantasy. In Psalm 77, the psalmist reflected on the Lord's presence during some of the darkest, most turbulent moments of his nation's history. "Your path led through the sea," he recalled, "your way through the mighty waters, though your footprints were not seen" (verse 19). In other words, "We couldn't see You or feel You in those heartbreaking, terrifying moments, but looking back, it's very clear that You led us and protected us every step of the way."

GOING DEEPER . . .

Jerusalem says, "The LORD has deserted us;
the LORD has forgotten us."

"Never! Can a mother forget her nursing child?
Can she feel no love for the child she has borne?
But even if that were possible,
I would not forget you!
See, I have written your name on
the palms of my hands."

ISAIAH 49:14-16, NLT

Have you ever jotted down a phone number on your own hand because you were in a pinch, needed to remember it, and couldn't find a scrap of paper? Our God has no such memory problems, but to help you understand His constant attention and love, He tells you that He has written your name on the palm of His hand. Carry that mental picture with you into your day . . . and your night.

— DAY 2 —
A Long Time

"ONE WHO WAS THERE had been an invalid for thirty-eight years. When Jesus saw him lying there and learned that he had been in this condition for a long time . . ." (John 5:5-6).

A few months from now, I will mark an anniversary that is at once a heartbreaking story of loss and an incomparable testimony of God's faithfulness. As of July this year, I will have been in a wheelchair for forty-seven years.

Forty-seven years, when compared to the Roman

lighthouse at Dover Castle or the pyramids, isn't much time at all. It's barely a heartbeat in history, and as nothing compared with eternity. But for a flesh-and-blood, earth-dwelling human being, forty-seven years in a wheelchair is a long time. Trust me on this: 17,155 days of quadriplegia are a great plenty.

Even Jesus thinks so. When He saw the paralyzed man lying on his mat at the pool of Bethesda, and learned that he had been in that condition thirty-eight years, He understood it to be "a long time."

You have no idea how much I value that phrase in Scripture. "A long time." The Lord of all, the One who existed eternally before time, who created time but lives outside of it, whose name is Ancient of Days and Everlasting God, *that* Jesus feels that living without the use of your legs for thirty-eight years—or forty-seven years—is a long time.

When the Savior's eyes rested on the paralyzed man lying on his worn, weathered straw mat, His heart went out to him. He saw more than a disabled man waiting through the years for healing, without any real hope. He took time to learn that poor soul's story. We can imagine Him whispering the words to Himself, "Thirty-eight years," and feeling the weight of those years in Himself.

In our Lord's humanity, thirty-eight years was more than His whole earthly life span. He understands time not only as something He created but also in an experiential, human way as well. As the book of Hebrews reminds us, "We don't have a priest who is out of touch with our reality" (Hebrews 4:15, MSG).

The God who is above time, beyond time, and outside of time chose to enter time, proving that He fully understands our experience of it. He knows how it feels to us when prayers seem to go unanswered . . . when pain or illness lingers . . . when days pass with no word from a loved one . . . when the pregnancy test keeps coming up negative . . . when we're stuck in a dreary, going-nowhere place in life. If it feels like "a long time" to us, we can count on it feeling that way to Him, too. It may be difficult for us to wait, but He waits with us, offering His own presence and companionship to see us through.

GOING DEEPER . . .

*Now that we know what we have—Jesus, this great
High Priest with ready access to God—let's not let it
slip through our fingers. We don't have a priest who
is out of touch with our reality. He's been through
weakness and testing, experienced it all—all but the
sin. So let's walk right up to him and get what he
is so ready to give. Take the mercy, accept the help.*

HEBREWS 4:14-16, MSG

From where you sit today, what things in your life seem to be taking "a long time"? Ask the Lord to kneel with you as He knelt with the man at the pool of Bethesda, to feel your frustration and fading hope, and to sustain you with His perspective, gift you with His incomparable peace, and empower you with His patience, so much richer and deeper than your own.

I CAN'T BEGIN to describe the feeling that swept over me shortly after my diving accident, when I realized I was a quadriplegic—that my paralysis was total and complete. Devastation? Depression? Denial? None of those terms even come close. The permanence of my condition was too much reality to bear.

It didn't help that my friends were going off to college, getting jobs, and going on dates while I was stuck in a hospital bed. My future? In a wheelchair? I couldn't bear to contemplate it. I cried out to God. I wanted reassurance that my world wasn't ripping apart at the seams. I longed for someone to promise that everything would be okay.

This is the heartfelt plea of anyone who suffers. We want assurance that somehow, someway, things will work out in the end, though we can't imagine how. We want to know that our world is orderly and stable, not spinning off into nightmarish chaos. We want to know that God is at the center of our suffering, not only holding our lives together but also holding us.

In Romans 8 we have the massive promise of that assurance: "And we know that for those who love God all things work together for good, for those who are called according to his purpose" (verse 28, ESV). In other words, the Lord is so supremely in charge of the world that everything touching our lives as Christians is ordered in such a way that it serves our good. This is true whether we face cancer, broken relationships, job loss, bankruptcy . . . or even a broken neck at age seventeen. The strong hope of the believer is not that we will escape "bad things" in the course of our lives, but that God will transform every one of our hardships into an instrument of His mercy to do us good.

That assurance goes way beyond the promise that "everything will be okay." Romans 8:29 reveals a far more stunning, mind-boggling purpose than that: Through our sufferings, we are being shaped into the very image of God's Son, Jesus Christ.

You need not panic or be swept away over your problems and setbacks. Paul said your sufferings are small and short when compared with the weight of glory they are accruing for you in heaven. So bear with heartbreak and hardship a bit longer. These things are expanding your soul's capacity for joy, worship, and service in heaven more than you can begin to imagine. "We must wait patiently and confidently" (Romans 8:25, NLT). Wait and trust in the Lord. Your present hope and expectation will not disappoint you.

GOING DEEPER . . .

*In face of all this, what is there left to say? If God
is for us, who can be against us? He that did not
hesitate to spare his own Son but gave him up for us
all—can we not trust such a God to give us, with
him, everything else that we can need? . . . I have
become absolutely convinced that neither death
nor life, neither messenger of Heaven nor monarch
of earth, neither what happens today nor what
may happen tomorrow, neither a power from on
high nor a power from below, nor anything else in
God's whole world has any power to separate us
from the love of God in Jesus Christ our Lord!*

ROMANS 8:31-32,38-39, PH

Stop and consider how God has transformed your hardships into instruments of needed change in your life. Don't allow today's trials and worries, large and intimidating as they might appear to be now, to overwhelm the reality of God's care, His ability to transform your situation, and His unshakable plan for good in your life.

— DAY 4 —
Show Me How to Live!

How ARE WE to deal with specific, repeated, heartfelt prayers that seem to go unanswered? We can allow ourselves to be worn down by our discouragement, leaving us dull and defeated, or we can focus our hope on Him alone, keeping the flame of faith bright and alive, believing that He is working day by day on our behalf and for our ultimate good.

For months after my injury at age seventeen, I kept waiting and waiting for "something supernatural" to stir in my life, bringing me a miraculous healing from paralysis. Not long after I was released from the hospital in Maryland, my sister Jay and I attended a Kathryn Kuhlman healing crusade in Washington, DC, at the Washington Hilton ballroom. The ushers escorted me to the wheelchair section, where I sat amongst dozens of other men and women with a variety of physical challenges. When the organ crescendoed, Kathryn Kuhlman swept out onstage in a spotlight, and everyone in our section got so excited. It seemed that people were getting healed around the auditorium, and I remember feeling like I was back at the pool of Bethesda, shouting, "Jesus, come over here! In the wheelchair section! Heal us, too!"

But then the meeting was over, we were escorted out, and I found myself in a long line of disappointed people on crutches and in wheelchairs, waiting at the elevators. What now? How could I go on like this? Why hadn't He healed me? All too soon, a bitter root—an angry, negative spirit of complaining—began to get a grip on my heart. In the midst of all the sulks and bitterness, Christ the Healer seemed so far away, so distant from me.

Finally, one night in the darkness I cried, "Oh, God, I can't live this way! Please, if I'm not going to die, You're just going to have to show me how to live!" That was my first plea for help, a cry in the darkness for God's peace and a sense of His purpose for my life. But it opened up much brighter days when my sister would come into the bedroom, open the drapes, set me up in the wheelchair, wheel me into the living room, and park my chair in front of a music stand holding a big Bible. With a rubber-tipped stick in my mouth, I would sit there all day, flipping through the pages of the Bible this way and that, trying to make sense of it all.

The truth is God had heard my cry that night, and He began a supernatural process of healing that would be so very much deeper than physical healing, drawing me closer to Himself in ways that would never have been possible otherwise. He may not always say yes to specific requests at specific times, but He will always say yes to the cry of a hungry heart that needs Him more than anything else. He longs to show us how to live at greater and greater levels of dependence on Him.

GOING DEEPER . . .

I'm feeling terrible—I couldn't feel worse!
Get me on my feet again.
You promised, remember? . . .
My sad life's dilapidated, a falling-down barn;
build me up again by your Word. . . .
I grasp and cling to whatever you tell me;
GOD, don't let me down!
I'll run the course you lay out for me
if you'll just show me how.

PSALM 119:25,28,31-32, MSG

Whatever your circumstances today, whatever the specific needs and concerns of your heart, pour them out before the Lord. He WILL answer, and the depth, wisdom, love, and timing He will show you in response to your cry for help will be so much more than you could have ever designed for yourself.

The Highest Priority

JESUS HEALED MANY PEOPLE during His time on earth. But He didn't heal everyone. Not even desperate men and women within a scant quarter mile of Him, waiting for His supernatural touch. The first chapter of Mark shows Jesus performing miracle after miracle for great crowds of sick and diseased people throughout the day and long past sunset. The next morning the needy crowds returned, but where was Jesus? Simon and his companions finally found Him praying in a solitary place. But when Simon

told Him about the needy and disabled multitude waiting down at the bottom of the hill, Jesus replied, "Let
us go somewhere else—to the nearby villages—so I can
preach there also. That is why I have come" (verse 38).

What? "Go somewhere else"? Jesus would actually
turn away from people who needed healing to preach
the message of the kingdom? I remember feeling stung
by that realization. If physical healing wasn't His priority, where did that leave me? In those days, what I
wanted most from Jesus was a quick fix for my pains,
problems, and paralysis. As time went by, however, I
began to see the bigger picture: Yes, Jesus cares about
suffering and spent most of His time on earth trying to
relieve it. But that wasn't why He came. This man who
healed sightless eyes and withered hands is the same
man who said, "If your eye causes you to sin, gouge it
out. If your hand causes you to sin, cut it off." In other
words, while physical healing might be a big deal, healing of the soul is even bigger.

That is when I began searching for a deeper healing, a
Psalm 139 kind of healing: "Search me, God, and know

my heart; test me and know my anxious thoughts. See if there is any offensive way in me, and lead me in the way everlasting" (verses 23-24).

For the last nearly half century in my wheelchair, that has been my prayer. And God has been answering, exposing dark corners of my heart that desperately need His healing light. God is still searching, testing, trying . . . and leading me in the way everlasting.

Does the Lord care about our disappointments and pain? Of course He does! The apostle Peter urged us to "cast all your anxiety on him because he cares for you" (1 Peter 5:7). Even so, He never promised to remove all of the hardships we face. No, there will be times when He allows them, purposes them, permits them, and even ordains them for our good. His highest priority is not our comfort or temporary prosperity, but the healing of our sin-damaged soul. Sometimes that divine therapy hurts, feels uncomfortable, or seems inconvenient. But it is the very best plan for our lives, conceived by Someone who loved us ten million years before we ever came to be.

GOING DEEPER . . .

*That's why we can be so sure that every detail
in our lives of love for God is worked into
something good. God knew what he was doing
from the very beginning. He decided from the
outset to shape the lives of those who love him
along the same lines as the life of his Son.*

ROMANS 8:28-29, MSG

There are no random events in the lives of God's
dearly loved, highly prized sons and daughters.
Everything—even the most difficult things—will
fit into a pattern for our good. He works behind
us, ahead of us, beneath us, above us, and within
us. No matter how we view ourselves, we are a
masterpiece of His grace.

– DAY 6 –
Because I Can't Be Trusted

Near the end of my stay in the hospital, friends would try their best to "explain" why God hadn't restored the use of my hands and legs. One friend said, "Joni, God knows He can trust you with suffering. He knows your character. He knows you're a strong person and you'll respond well to hardships."

I hate to break anyone's bubble here, but that idea's about as flimsy as a bubble. In fact, the very opposite is true: I think God entrusts me with hardships because He knows very well that I can't be trusted. I fully accept the fact that I am the least likely candidate to handle affliction well. Honestly, I know all too well how weak and stubborn I can be, how peevish, moody, and irritable. And this is why I run to God daily—hourly—for help! Oh, help me, Jesus. I can't do this. I can't face one more day of quadriplegia. I can't handle one more hour of this chronic, razor-sharp pain. I can't hold onto hope while the shadow of cancer lingers!

When I go to God with that attitude, He lavishes grace upon grace on me. Why does He do it? Because I'm very quick to recognize my weakness and reach out for a double handful of His strength.

One of David's finest moments came at an unlikely spot on the biblical map called Ziklag. At this point in his life, he was an outlaw warrior leading a rough-hewn band of fugitives, malcontents, and rebels. One day, after returning from a raid, David and his men found that their own town had been ransacked, raided, and burned to the ground. Worse still, their wives and children had been kidnapped. The Bible says that David and his men "wept aloud until they had no strength left to weep" (1 Samuel 30:4). Just that quickly, David's ragtag army turned against him and talked about stoning him to death.

What did David do? He didn't walk, he ran, into the arms of his God. The text says, "But David strengthened himself in the Lord his God" (30:6, ESV). A short time later, he rose from his knees with courage restored—and with a fresh plan for victory.

That's what I do. In my incredible weakness, I "strengthen myself" in the Lord. When despair threatens to overtake me, I immediately reach up for a double handful of hope from heaven. God can trust me to do that, and He never fails to respond.

If you desire the favor of God today, be swift to appreciate how out of favor you would be apart from Christ. If you want the strength of God, be faster than anyone else to realize how feeble and ridiculously needy you are without Christ.

When it comes to dealing daily with suffering, it really is all about Jesus.

GOING DEEPER . . .

*By faith these people overthrew kingdoms,
ruled with justice, and received what God
had promised them. They shut the mouths of
lions, quenched the flames of fire, and escaped
death by the edge of the sword. Their weakness
was turned to strength. They became strong
in battle and put whole armies to flight.*

HEBREWS 11:33-34, NLT

*I am ready for anything through the
strength of the one who lives within me.*

PHILIPPIANS 4:13, PH

No matter how weak, inadequate, clueless, or unworthy you may feel right now, you can fall before the Lord and reach out for a double handful of His strength, wisdom, and perspective. Don't hesitate or hold back or live in a world of denial that insists "I can handle this on my own." You can't! RUN to your Father for help.

— DAY 7 —
Thanks-Making

GIVING THANKS TO GOD for my life and the events of my days may come supernaturally to me now, but it wasn't always this way.

After I was released from the hospital, my sister invited me to come live with her on our Maryland farm. Still a teenager and new to my wheelchair, I wondered what my new life as a quadriplegic would be. Often, my sister parked me in my chair next to the big bay window that overlooked the pasture. Everything in me wanted to be on my feet, outside, walking into the barn, feeding the horses, and saddling up for a ride.

And yes, at that moment I was feeling very sorry for myself.

But even in those days I knew that daydreaming and fantasizing about such things would only make my attitude worse. I'd had enough of dark depression when I was in the hospital and didn't want to go down that grim path to despair again. So sitting there by the window, looking out at the morning sunlight on that Maryland pasture, I remember praying a prayer that went something like this:

"Jesus, my mind-set today is like a stubborn horse that doesn't want to be saddled up and led out of the barn. My attitude is stiff-necked and obstinate—but I am not going to let it win this day. My spirit within me wants to do what's right, so I'm putting spurs on my attitude today. I'm going to goad it out of the barn, into the light of day, and down a path of gratitude. My feelings don't want to go there; I'd rather stay in my dark stall. But with Your help, I'm going to whip my feelings in the right direction. And as I do . . . please, Lord, give me a grateful attitude. Help me not only to do but also to feel the right thing."

I wanted God to shed His light on a new path.

And He did.

Over time, God changed those feelings and gave me an attitude of genuine, heartfelt gratitude. Nothing or no one else could have changed me from the inside out like that. It had to be me in partnership with God's powerful Holy Spirit.

Does thankfulness come easy to you today? Do you have an attitude that wants to hide in a dark stall in the back of the barn, or one that wills to ride in the morning sunlight on a fresh trail? It may be time to spur your emotions in the right direction. In 2 Corinthians 4:15, Paul wrote, "All this is for your benefit, so that the grace that is reaching more and more people may cause thanksgiving to overflow to the glory of God." In other words, when you cultivate an attitude of gratitude, it causes others to be thankful. As a friend of mine often says, "We can actually become thanks-makers."

And that sounds like a pretty good occupation to me.

GOING DEEPER . . .

*I will sacrifice a thank offering to you
and call on the name of the LORD.*

PSALM 116:17

*Our constant sacrifice to God should be the
praise of lips that give thanks to his name.*

HEBREWS 13:15, PH

Drawing on the power of the Holy Spirit, encourage your own heart to give thanks right now . . . inspiring and encouraging others in your life to do the same, all of it overflowing to the glory of God. This may be the most important thing you accomplish all day.

As a Thousand Years

LOOKING BACK, there was one good thing about my time in the hospital: My days had structure. There were physical therapy sessions and vocational rehab, occupational therapy and lab appointments. But on the farm, the hours drifted by without real aim or purpose. Occasionally, I would fall back into depressed feelings. My friend Steve saw this on one of his visits and gave me a simple but powerful Bible verse that guided me through the toughest days ahead: "But do not forget this one thing, dear friends: With the Lord a day is like a thousand years, and a thousand years are like a day" (2 Peter 3:8).

We've all heard the adage that God looks at the last two thousand years as a couple of days gone by, but what about viewing each day as a thousand years? If we saw each day as comparable to a millennium in eternity, we'd understand that each twenty-four hours is chock-full of opportunities to invest in a thousand years' worth of eternity. Each day God gives us the precious gift of hours to invest in the lives of others—investments that will have eternal repercussions for us and for them.

I perked up when Steve shared this idea. "Yes," I said, "but I'm still in a wheelchair. I can't do all the things I used to do. How can my life count in this condition?" Shooting up a quick prayer for wisdom, Steve told me, "First, Joni, you can pray. No matter how feeble or faint-hearted your prayers may seem, they have very special power with God. Now is your chance to stretch your soul's capacity for God. Your patience and endurance will resound more to God's glory than you can possibly imagine right now."

"But sometimes I still feel like giving up," I sighed.

Steve said, "Even Jesus thought of others when He was on His deathbed—the cross. We are always called to think of others, no matter how difficult our circumstances. You can make your days count by focusing on your family, thanking and encouraging them and finding ways to bless them. Who knows how many years of eternal benefit—hundreds? thousands?—it will pan out to be for you, your family, and the glory of God?"

The next day I got started. I remembered to thank my sister for getting me into my wheelchair that morning. I wrote a note of encouragement to a sick relative. I decided to memorize a Scripture once a week. I called a friend and prayed with her on the phone. I invited Steve and his friends to start a Bible study at our farmhouse. And I made sure to give my family a smile instead of a frown. After a month and a half or so, I was able to look on those forty-five days as forty-five thousand years' worth of eternal blessing to others, benefit to me, and glory to God. Those weeks became the most meaningful and important ones I had lived thus far in my wheelchair.

With 2 Peter 3:8 tucked in my belt, something changed, and in a big way. I was ready to wheel into a much brighter future.

God, the Creator of time, knows how to invest the days and hours of our lives with mighty significance. In His wisdom and with His favor, your words and acts of compassion and faith today can have an impact far, far beyond twenty-four hours.

GOING DEEPER . . .

Teach us to number our days,
that we may gain a heart of wisdom.

PSALM 90:12

In other words, value your days—this day—and make the most of every opportunity to do good, because this is the wisdom God wants you to apply to your twenty-four-hour slices of time. No wonder the Bible describes each day as like a thousand years—that's how priceless they are!

The Day's First Battle

THERE ARE MOMENTS at the dawn of each new day, brief seconds in the transition between sleep and waking, when great battles are won or lost.

Just this morning, in those in-between moments of waking from sleep but not yet opening my eyes, I had a decision to make. Can I face this day? Do I have the energy? Can I muster the strength? In those fleeting seconds, I had to choose what kind of day it would be. Would it be a good day? Would I place my trust in the Lord for strength?

If you're not sixty-four years old and quadriplegic, it's difficult to explain. But when you lie in one position all night, unable to move, it makes the whole prospect of waking up so . . . unappealing. Some days it seems like scaling a mountain, and my mind shrinks away from it. Sometimes I simply don't want to face one more day of paralysis and chronic pain.

This morning, however, with the covers still pulled up and my eyes still closed, I connected with the Lord Jesus, who neither slumbers nor sleeps. *Lord Jesus, there are a zillion things I need to catch up on today: an appointment with the oncologist, a radio interview, a staff meeting, a dinner commitment. And Lord, my emotions are telling me I don't want to do ANY of it. But I know that if I give in to my feelings, I will end up on a dark, discouraged, defeated path. Lord, help me! I don't want that! So Lord, right now by faith I'm laying claim to Psalm 79:8: "May your mercy come quickly to meet us, for we are in desperate need." Lord, I claim that verse. I own it, I embrace it, and I believe You will give me, right now, all the grace available through it!*

All of that flashed through my mind and soul in just

seconds. And when I opened my eyes on the day . . . I had grace. I can't explain it, but it was there. I had the grace of God and the God of all grace on my side. I had unmerited favor streaming straight from heaven, filling my heart with courage and giving me His perspective.

If there is one thing God wants for you and me in those first waking moments, it is the realization of our victory in Jesus. We are not to feel defeated before the day begins. He wants us to be victorious right from the get-go, to be more than conquerors. And with that realization, He wants us to extend the same grace we have received to others in our world who may be experiencing defeat and discouragement.

GOING DEEPER . . .

Listen to my cry,
for I am in desperate need;
rescue me from those who pursue me,
for they are too strong for me.
Set me free from my prison,
that I may praise your name.
Then the righteous will gather about me
because of your goodness to me.

PSALM 142:6-7

But I will sing of your strength,
in the morning I will sing of your love;
for you are my fortress,
my refuge in times of trouble.

PSALM 59:16

Join me in making those few brief seconds in the morning before you open your eyes a time of prayer—short, sincere, and from the heart. You will be amazed by the supernatural attitude God gives you for the day.

— DAY 10 —
When You Are Squeezed

KEN AND I recently celebrated thirty-one years of marriage. But with my quadriplegia and the frustrating, constant pain that has shadowed me for the last ten years, every step has required a tough, earnest, rugged, rigorous reliance on Jesus Christ.

Even in marriage? Especially in marriage. Even though my wonderful, godly husband thought he knew what he'd signed up for when he married a paralyzed woman in a wheelchair, he really didn't. As the years went by, the dreary, nonstop, 24-7, day-to-day routines associated with my level of disability began to weigh on him. Then, when the severe, seemingly inexplicable pain entered my experience, it was almost (as the expression goes) "a bridge too far." Little by little, Ken slipped into a deep, numbing depression. As a result, I began to pull back emotionally too. It hurt so much to see my disability cause my husband such pain. These were what we look back on now as the "tired middle years" of our marriage.

It was a difficult time for both of us, and we wished that God would just lift all the burdens and wash away the disappointment, struggle, and emotional pain of those days. But God had a different plan in mind. In fact, He used those trials and that pressure to squeeze us, revealing the selfish, spiteful ways that were still too prominent in our hearts and in our character. In time, those difficult circumstances pushed us into a whole new level of dependence on Christ—in our marriage, and in everything else.

Quite frankly, I don't like to be squeezed like a lemon. I don't like it when heartbreaks, stress, and failures reveal the darker, still-unchanged parts of my soul. But I do like what happens when I cast myself afresh on the strength, love, presence, enabling, and sufficiency of Jesus Christ. The more Ken and I clung to Jesus during those days (as circumstances went from bad to worse), the more our marriage began to heal, becoming stronger, sweeter, more intimate, and more joyful than we had ever experienced. God was doing a deep-down healing in both of us, and we have discovered a love that holds on through it all. We have learned that the strongest relationships don't come easy; they are earned. They are tested by pain and frustration, and sometimes they are pushed to what feels like the breaking point. But if those hardships push us into a profound, openhanded dependence on God's Son, He will bring great and unexpected good out of even the worst of it.

As the psalmist said, "You have turned for me my mourning into dancing; you have loosed my sackcloth and clothed me with gladness" (Psalm 30:11, ESV).

GOING DEEPER . . .

I was given a physical condition which has been a thorn in my flesh, a messenger from Satan to hurt and bother me and prick my pride. Three different times I begged God to make me well again.

Each time he said, "No. But I am with you; that is all you need. My power shows up best in weak people." Now I am glad to boast about how weak I am; I am glad to be a living demonstration of Christ's power, instead of showing off my own power and abilities. Since I know it is all for Christ's good, I am quite happy about "the thorn," and about insults and hardships, persecutions and difficulties; for when I am weak, then I am strong—the less I have, the more I depend on him.

2 CORINTHIANS 12:7-10, TLB

Remember, at your weakest, most vulnerable moment you are never nearer to the unlimited, inexhaustible power and love of the living Christ. Reach out your hand—and if you can't manage that, just lift your little finger. Whatever your need, however dire it may seem, He will meet you with the resources of heaven.

— DAY 11 —

Joyful in Hope

FORCED BED REST has never been high on my list of favorite activities.

If I needed any reminding of that fact, it came back to me when I read an e-mail from my new friend Jennifer, a fourteen-year-old ventilator-dependent quadriplegic who has a nasty pressure sore. The ulcer has gotten so deep that she can no longer sit up in her wheelchair. The doctor has assigned her to bed . . . for the next four months.

My heart goes out to Jen. When she was three years

old, an improperly anchored swing set toppled over on her, paralyzing her instantly. Over the years, Jennifer has struggled with ups and downs. But in this e-mail she asked for my advice, knowing I've "been there" with stubborn pressure sores of my own.

"Jennifer," I wrote back to her, "one of the things you must do is stay focused. Don't let your mind wander into depression and boredom. I have a secret that helps me: I choose a Bible verse and memorize it. In fact, during a recent four-week stint in bed, I picked Romans 12:12: 'Be joyful in hope, patient in affliction, faithful in prayer.'"

Joyful in hope? It isn't easy for Jennifer right now. She doesn't want to be paralyzed . . . doesn't want to be on a ventilator just to stay alive . . . and certainly doesn't relish the idea of lying in bed for sixteen straight weeks.

Why is it so difficult to be joyful in hope? Because the focus of our hope is yet to be fulfilled. We don't yet possess, or even see, that for which we hope. When I was in bed for four weeks, it hit home that God wants me to be joyful about future things in spite of my present circumstances. The secret is embracing what lies just over the heavenly horizon: One day soon there will be no more pain, tears, or sorrow. No more death, disease, or disability. Peace will flow, wide and deep as the Columbia River, joy will spring up like an artesian fountain, and we will reign with King Jesus forever.

Does the idea of the Lord's return and heavenly glories put a smile on your face? Heaven will seem near and real as you stir up your joy over that in which you hope. Join me and my friend Jennifer today in staying focused. Ask the Lord to stir a lively vision of heaven in your heart. Before long the joy of the Lord will overtake you. Just five minutes in heaven will suffice for all of earth's hurts. Jennifer's four months in bed—in fact, her whole life of disability and paralysis—will melt away like a dream as light from an eternal morning streams into her window.

GOING DEEPER . . .

Take a good look at me, GOD, my God;
I want to look life in the eye,
So no enemy can get the best of me
or laugh when I fall on my face.

I've thrown myself headlong into your arms—
I'm celebrating your rescue.
I'm singing at the top of my lungs,
I'm so full of answered prayers.

PSALM 13:3-6, MSG

But now, Lord, what do I look for?
My hope is in you.

PSALM 39:7

Pray with me: Lord, if You want me to have joy growing out of real hope, and it takes a long, hard road to get there . . . then I know it's for my own good, and that's what I want too. But You will have to help me, because when the pain comes, when boredom invades, when discouragement creeps into the room, I so often lose my focus. Oh, Lord Jesus, lift my sight to the wonders of the home You have prepared for me . . . just around the corner, just over the horizon. Amen.

— DAY 12 —
The Source of Our Courage

ONE MORNING, Ken and I were about to head out to our offices at Joni and Friends when he caught a look in my eyes and perceived that I had a physically painful day ahead of me.

He opened the front door, then stopped in his tracks. "Wait one moment!" he said, and ran back into the house. He came back with a large yellow sticky note on which he had inscribed a big capital *C* with a black marker. Then he placed it on my chest, over my heart.

"What's this?" I asked.

"It's *C* for Courage. You've got courage, Joni. I can see it in your eyes. You're going to make it today. You're going to do it, and I am praying for you. You've got the courage of Christ."

Oh, my goodness, what encouraging, hopeful words to hear from my husband. As strange as it may sound, he and I are grateful for the disability, for the chronic pain, and yes, even for the cancer that invaded our lives in 2010. Why? Because we're masochists who enjoy suffering? No, of course not. It's because all of these things help us stay hungry for the bread of heaven and thirsty for the living water. They remind us that courage doesn't flow from our own reservoirs of strength and character, but from the living Christ who makes His home within us. Our own wells of courage might be dry as dust, but the courage of Jesus flows on—leaping, sparkling, and fresh—like a spring-fed mountain stream.

Our bouts with physical or emotional suffering keep waking us up out of any spiritual slumber we might find ourselves in. Trouble and hardship are textbooks that repeatedly instruct us who we really are, and remind us that we aren't the towers of strength or paradigms of virtue we sometimes like to imagine we are. Suffering sandblasts us, stripping us of our sinful ways, leaving us raw and exposed—so that we might be better bonded to the Savior.

The best courage in times of crisis isn't the kind we siphon out of the tepid, shallow pools at the bottom of our soul. For one thing, that courage will never last! The best courage is the kind that has been channeled from heaven itself—a vast reservoir wider than the human mind can conceive.

Knowing God is ecstasy beyond compare. Walking with His Son, Jesus, is ecstasy beyond compare. Hear me on this: It is worth anything to be His friend. Anything. No matter what the hardship. No matter how long or steep the road.

The capital *C* Ken put on my chest that morning was intended to represent the word *courage*, but it was really more about the hour-by-hour, moment-after-moment companionship of God's Son.

GOING DEEPER . . .

For my people have done two evil things:
They have abandoned me—
the fountain of living water.
And they have dug for themselves cracked cisterns
that can hold no water at all!

JEREMIAH 2:13, NLT

Think of fear and faltering confidence as bright orange road signs reminding us to tap into the limitless courage of Christ. The sooner we realize (and admit) our need, the sooner we can receive His provision of help and renewed hope.

A Fleeting Moment

KEN AND I are well into our sixties, and up until now we haven't talked much about dying. It was always something "we'll discuss later, when we're older." That changed several years ago when I was diagnosed with stage three breast cancer. Suddenly, the frightening prospect we never dared to broach became a looming possibility. With my fragile condition as a quadriplegic, I might not make it through chemotherapy. And the chemo might not kill all the cancer. I might . . . die.

The thought terrified Ken. My sister, who stayed with us to help me through chemotherapy, caught him crying one day in the kitchen. He put down the sponge and dish, turned to her with wet eyes, and said, "I might lose her. I might lose my best friend."

After the episode at the sink, I noticed a change. Ken and I sat outside in the backyard more often, enjoying the breeze and the birds at the feeder. We noticed small things: tiny flowers poking through the soil, the pleasant sound of water in the fountain, a little lizard scurrying by. We talked more, sharing memories of favorite vacations. We visited the beach. Prayed hand in hand more frequently. Read books together. Discussed God and opened the Bible together. In short, our love for each other deepened, as well as our vision of heaven.

Ken and I are thankful for our scare with cancer. It awakened us to how fragile life is—and how quickly it passes. King David had a similar experience. In Psalm 39 he wrote, "LORD, remind me how brief my time on earth will be. Remind me that my days are numbered—how fleeting my life is. You have made my life no longer than the width of my hand. My entire lifetime is just a moment to you; at best, each of us is but a breath" (verses 4-5, NLT).

Our afflictions underscore how frail and tenuous our life on earth really is. Old age and disability lift our eyes off this earth and force us to think about life eternal, where there is no sorrow or pain. We are not as strong as we tell ourselves; our mind may try to convince us otherwise, but we are not invincible.

God's measuring rod of your life on earth is summed up in a single word: *fleeting!* We are but a moment. . . . He is eternal. We must be made to agree with God's assessment of our lives and learn to yield to His purposes.

GOING DEEPER . . .

We are merely moving shadows,
and all our busy rushing ends in nothing.
We heap up wealth,
not knowing who will spend it.
And so, LORD, where do I put my hope?
My only hope is in you.

PSALM 39:6-7, NLT

Now listen, you who say, "Today or tomorrow we
will go to this or that city, spend a year there, carry
on business and make money." Why, you do not even
know what will happen tomorrow. What is your
life? You are a mist that appears for a little while
and then vanishes. Instead, you ought to say, "If it is
the LORD's will, we will live and do this or that."

JAMES 4:13-15

One reason God wants us to understand the brevity of life is to redirect us to the next life, the joyful, never-ending life beyond the grave, waiting for us in heaven. This life is not the only life there is, nor is it the main thing. There's a much bigger and forever-longer life on the horizon! That's a very good thing to know, of course, but don't file the truth away in some dusty mental file cabinet. THINK about it today. Turn it over in your mind. Let the happy truth seep into every corner of your soul.

— DAY 14 —
The Glory of a New Heart

DAY BY DAY, God still searches, tests, and tries me, as Psalm 139:24 says, seeing "if there is any offensive way in me," and leading me "in the way everlasting." That is why you will often find me quoting from memory the general confession from the Book of Common Prayer, which I memorized as a young child growing up in the Reformed Episcopal Church:

Almighty and most merciful Father, we have erred and strayed from Thy ways. We have followed too much the devices and the desires

of our own hearts. We have offended against
Thy holy laws. We have left undone those things
which we ought to have done, and we have done
those things which we ought not to have done;
and there is no health in us.

I love that confession, but I also hate that confession.
I love the old familiar words and many of the memories
that accompany them. But it's a grief to me that this
confession remains so true of my own heart. Too often,
it is an accurate snapshot of my soul, and I long for the
day when it will finally (and forever) change. Over the
years, I have written quite a bit about the life to come
and how much I look forward to a new body that jumps,
dances, runs, and crunches through autumn leaves on
heaven's country lanes. And yes, that will be glorious
beyond words—a great fringe benefit of being invited to
Christ's coronation party. But that's not what I'm looking
forward to most.

I want a new heart. I want a changed heart that fits
right into heaven. I want a heart that no longer twists

the truth, resists God, looks for escapes, gets defeated by pain, tries to justify itself, or becomes anxious and worried about the future. That will be heaven for me. As the old hymn says, "Oh, that will be glory for me, glory for me, glory for me, when by His grace I shall look on His face."

It will be glory to have a new heart, and it is glory today—right now—to have a heart renewed and made clean by Jesus Christ. This is the message our ministry brings to hundreds of thousands of suffering people. People with disabilities. Diseased, injured, sick people who have longed for physical healing but never received it. There is profound, deep-down-to-the-soul healing in Jesus. As James 3:2 says, "We all stumble in many ways," but there is forgiveness, release, and an almost-indescribable renewal in a relationship with the living Son of God. And in the heaven to come, that healing will be permanent.

GOING DEEPER . . .

If you, LORD, kept a record of sins,
LORD, who could stand?
But with you there is forgiveness,
so that we can, with reverence, serve you.

I wait for the LORD, my whole being waits,
and in his word I put my hope.

PSALM 130:3-5

If we refuse to admit that we are sinners, then
we live in a world of illusion and truth becomes
a stranger to us. But if we freely admit that we
have sinned, we find God utterly reliable and
straightforward—he forgives our sins and makes
us thoroughly clean from all that is evil.

1 JOHN 1:8-9, PH

Think of all the clean things you love most: clean sheets . . . crisp, clean clothing . . . a clean, shiny house . . . a sparkling clean car, right out of the carwash . . . a clean, windswept blue sky . . . the clean white of fresh-fallen snow. Now take time to think about the miracle of a heart washed totally clean by the blood of Jesus Christ, shed for us on the cross. Praise Him and thank Him for the price He paid to make that possible.

A Splash of Heaven

KEN AND I were driving our van down the 101 freeway, coming home from yet another chemotherapy session. It was the kind of day many cancer patients would immediately recognize: I felt nauseous and utterly worn out. As we drove along, with Ken behind the wheel and me and my wheelchair secured in back, we were talking about suffering.

"It's like a splash-over of hell," I said. "It wakes us up out of our spiritual slumber and prompts us to remember what Christ rescued us from."

Ken met my eyes in the rearview mirror. I knew he had been suffering through this difficult season right along with me. "Remembering that rescue," he added, "creates gratitude in our hearts when we think about what Jesus has secured on our behalf."

It was quiet for a few miles as we turned off at our exit and headed down Cairnloch Street. Pulling into the driveway, Ken shut off the engine and turned to look at me. "Well then," he said. "If suffering is a splash-over of hell, what do you think a splash-over of heaven is?"

Good question, Ken! Was a splash-over of heaven one of those easy-breezy bright days when there are no bad medical reports, no pain, no nausea; when everything is going well, and life is comfortable and cozy?

No, that didn't sound right to either of us. What we finally agreed on was that a splash-over of heaven is finding Jesus in your splash-over of hell. As reluctant as we might have been to admit it at times, some of the best, sweetest, most intimate moments in our walk with Jesus have grown out of some of the darkest, most painful, and frightening times of our lives. They were moments when the Son of God came striding into our darkness, just as He once walked on the wild waves of the Sea of Galilee, approaching the boat of His friends in the teeth of a terrifying storm. To find Jesus in your hell, to find Him walking across the waves of your storm in the night with His hand outstretched, is a taste of heaven. Somehow, in the midst of your suffering, the Son of God beckons you into the inner sanctum of His own suffering—a place of mystery and privilege you will never forget. I have suffered, yes. But I wouldn't trade places with anybody in the world to be this close to Jesus.

GOING DEEPER . . .

Yes, everything else is worthless when compared
with the infinite value of knowing Christ
Jesus my Lord. . . . I want to know Christ and
experience the mighty power that raised him
from the dead. I want to suffer with him, sharing
in his death, so that one way or another I will
experience the resurrection from the dead!

PHILIPPIANS 3:8,10-11, NLT

Have you experienced a splash-over of hell in your life? Do you find yourself in a place of pressure, anxiety, disappointment, or pain that you never anticipated and don't know how you will survive, let alone handle? Just remember that, as difficult as it may seem to believe, there may be a splash-over of heaven on the heels of your heartache. No matter the situation or circumstance, the presence of Jesus changes everything.

Abiding in Christ

MY BONE DENSITY SCAN last week should have been a breeze . . . but it wasn't. For most patients, this medical test means slipping into a surgical gown, hopping on the table, and taking a ten-minute nap while the scanner does its thing.

But I'm not most patients.

To begin with, the scanner was in a tiny closet of a room, barely wide enough for my wheelchair. Heaving me onto the table was no easy feat; it took two men to do it. Then Ken nearly wrenched his back positioning my body in line with the machine. After the scan, it took way more time than you would think to get me dressed on the table and back into my wheelchair. When it was over, Ken and I were both exhausted.

After all these years, you would think quadriplegia would get easier. That it would begin to fit like an old slipper. But it doesn't. If anything, it gets more burdensome as the years go by. Through that whole ordeal at the doctor's, I was praying, "Oh, Lord, give us grace, give us grace. Jesus, oh, Lord, help us!" But then again, I always pray that way. My paralysis and my wheelchair have me constantly asking God for help. You sometimes hear people talk about "abiding in Christ" as if it were some super-saintly level of spiritual life. But for me, it's a daily, hourly necessity. I dare not separate myself from Jesus—my disability just won't allow it!

In John 15:5, Jesus said, "I am the vine; you are the branches. Whoever abides in me and I in him, he it is that bears much fruit, for apart from me you can do nothing" (ESV). In a recent blog, Joshua Harris reminded his readers that we're not like iPhones or iPads that need an occasional charge. No, we need to stay plugged into Jesus 24-7. Harris wrote, "Jesus doesn't say 'I am [the] power cord [and] you are the cell phone.' He says, 'I'm the vine. You're the branch.' [There's a huge difference.] . . . Abiding is what desperate people do who realize that they have no life, power, no inward resource of themselves."

That is the one great positive of quadriplegia. My disability makes me constantly aware that I am a totally dependent on Jesus. Branches don't separate themselves from the vine and live independent lives. No, a separated branch is a dying branch. Its leaves begin to wither immediately.

Branches are part of the Vine, and they're supposed to act like it. So, my friend, you be the branch that relaxes in, abides in, and draws strength from Jesus Christ, the true and living Vine.

GOING DEEPER . . .

But blessed are those who trust in the LORD
and have made the LORD their hope and confidence.
They are like trees planted along a riverbank,
with roots that reach deep into the water.
Such trees are not bothered by the heat
or worried by long months of drought.
Their leaves stay green,
and they never stop producing fruit.

JEREMIAH 17:7-8, NLT

Now choose life, so that you and your children
may live and that you may love the LORD
your God, listen to his voice, and hold fast
to him. For the LORD is your life.

DEUTERONOMY 30:19-20

Lord, thank You that You are my very life. My life is hidden in Yours. I draw my identity, my strength, my wisdom, my righteousness, my salvation, my hope, and my joy directly from You and nowhere else. In You I live and move and have my being. Forgive me for imagining I have some limited "battery life" and can live on my own for even one minute. I can't . . . and what's more, I don't want to. In Your strong name, Amen.

– DAY 17 –
Your Role in Eternity

"His INTENT was that now, through the church, the manifold wisdom of God should be made known to the rulers and authorities in the heavenly realms, according to his eternal purpose that he accomplished in Christ Jesus our Lord" (Ephesians 3:10-11).

This is one of those Bible passages that becomes more and more stunning and mind-boggling the longer you think about it. It's like a rock tossed into a perfectly still pool, with concentric rings of impact rolling out farther and farther.

The apostle Paul told us that God teaches the unseen world all about Himself, and He does so by using you and me as His audiovisual aids. In some manner beyond our present comprehension, the Lord chooses to use our earthly lives to show the universe the marvels and wonders of His grace and kindness in Christ. Let's imagine some demon would dare waltz up to heaven's throne and sneer, "God, people only trust You because You bless them with health and strength. But let me put a cancer in the body of some missionary lady. Then let me take away her financial support. Everyone knows what would happen: She would deny You to Your face!"

But God would answer, "Oh, no, you are wrong. That exact scenario happened to My servant Eliza Brown, and she trusted Me through it all. I worked through her obedience, and because of her radiant testimony many more people heard of My Son's salvation."

At that point the demon (acknowledging the undeniable truth of this) would slink away, and the glory surrounding God would glow even brighter. Eliza Brown's sufferings not only helped her grow in Christ but also demonstrated to that demon—and millions more like him—the limitless, transforming power of God's sustaining grace. The result? Greater glory to God. One day it will be shown to all that God was able to rescue sinners, redeem suffering, crush the rebellious, restore all things, vindicate His holy name, provide restitution . . . and come out all the more glorious for it. What an inexpressible honor to have a share in that!

Yes, I know, it's difficult to remember these truths when you suddenly find yourself mired in difficult or even heartbreaking circumstances. Even so, you have the opportunity in those moments to be like Eliza Brown. God will use your situation, however complicated, hurtful, or unfair it may seem right now, to build you up spiritually and to reveal stunning new facets of His glory even "to the rulers and authorities in the heavenly realms."

GOING DEEPER . . .

The purpose is that all the angelic powers
should now see the complex wisdom of God's
plan being worked out through the Church,
in conformity to that timeless purpose which
he centred in Christ Jesus, our Lord.

EPHESIANS 3:10,11, PH

For our present troubles are small and won't last
very long. Yet they produce for us a glory that
vastly outweighs them and will last forever! So
we don't look at the troubles we can see now;
rather, we fix our gaze on things that cannot be
seen. For the things we see now will soon be gone,
but the things we cannot see will last forever.

2 CORINTHIANS 4:17-18, NLT

Father, I recognize that my perspective is so narrow and small. It's like looking at the Milky Way through a pinhole! Please help me comprehend today just a little bit more of Your eternal plan and purpose in my life. And if You choose to use me as an audiovisual aid before the angels, help me bring honor to my Savior. In His strong name, Amen.

— DAY 18 —

Blessing Your Critics

WHEN JESUS SPOKE in His hometown synagogue, people could be seen shaking their heads and whispering behind their hands.

"Where did he get all this wisdom and the power to perform such miracles?"

"He's just a carpenter."

"Isn't He the son of Mary and the brother of James, Joseph, Judas, and Simon?"

"His sisters live right here among us."

The gospel of Mark says "they were deeply offended and

refused to believe in him" (6:3, NLT). Even His own brothers got into the act. In the John 7:2-10 account, I imagine Jesus walking into a room and His brothers suddenly pretending to look grave and serious (all the time suppressing grins and winking at one another). "Well, brother Jesus, don't You think You'd better show up at this important feast? After all, if You want to be taken seriously . . . if You want to be a public figure . . . You'd better make an appearance . . . circulate . . . talk to the right people."

John adds that "his brothers were pushing him like this because they didn't believe in him either" (7:5, MSG). John goes on to say, "Among the crowds there was widespread whispering about him. Some said . . . 'he deceives the people'" (verse 12).

Ironically, it was Jesus' goodness and kindness that got Him into trouble with people. In fact, it frightened them. One village asked Jesus to move on after He healed their town's most notorious psychotics. Others whom He greatly helped seemed too embarrassed or preoccupied to even turn and thank Him. Many avoided Him for fear of getting kicked out of their synagogues.

But this negative response never intimidated Jesus for a moment. He never backed down. He kept to the furrow He was plowing.

Have you ever found yourself the subject of gossip in your office or at school because of your witness for Christ? Do neighbors whisper behind your back? Have people winced or smiled stiffly at your words of witness and then said, "No thanks"? Have you ever felt left out at parties, or you're the last to be invited to sit at the "popular" table in the lunchroom? It's okay. It's what happened to Jesus many, many times in His earthly walk. Don't fret or feel intimidated. If Jesus kept to the furrow He was plowing, you must too. After all, you are the servant following in the Master's tracks.

Do what Jesus did. Bless those who shun you—bless, and don't think bad of them. Those who reject or disdain you around others may secretly be observing you very carefully. In a time of crisis, in a day of worry or danger or despair, it may very well be you they turn to, rather than their shallow, superficial "friends."

GOING DEEPER . . .

As for those who try to make your life a misery,
bless them. Don't curse, bless. Share the happiness
of those who are happy, the sorrow of those who are
sad. Live in harmony with each other. Don't become
snobbish but take a real interest in ordinary people.
Don't become set in your own opinions. Don't
pay back a bad turn by a bad turn, to anyone.

ROMANS 12:14-17, PH

Since you can't control how others respond to you, make it your aim to be positive, friendly, nondefensive, and interested in others. Rather than bringing attention to yourself, this will ultimately bring attention to your Lord. Let goodness and kindness be the rule in all your dealings with others, and He will get the glory.

God's Masterpiece

I REMEMBER visiting the Louvre in Paris, strolling with a group of friends through what seemed like miles of beautiful and incredibly valuable works of art. As we made our way into yet another corridor, I saw a gathering of people at the far end, apparently standing in front of a painting.

It must be famous, I thought, as we moved in for a closer look. And it was. It was Leonardo da Vinci's *Mona Lisa* . . . the mysterious lady with the enigmatic smile. And because this was such an invaluable work of art, the curators not only had put it behind glass to control the temperature and humidity but had also roped it off to keep people at a distance. There was even an armed and stern-looking security guard standing nearby.

The painting itself was relatively small, making it all but impossible to enjoy any details in da Vinci's work, because you had to keep your distance. Don't touch! Don't come near! Stand back!

But God treats His masterpieces quite differently. What or whom are His masterpieces? We are! God's redeemed sons and daughters. Ephesians 2:10 says, "For we are God's handiwork, created in Christ Jesus to do good works, which God prepared in advance for us to do." That word *handiwork* is the Greek word *poiema* and refers to God's workmanship, something He takes great delight in creating.

In a church service I attended not long ago, the pastor reminded us of this fact, and then invited us to stand up, reach out, and touch someone near us. "Give them a hug if you can," he said. "Shake their hands, give their shoulders a squeeze." Everyone happily complied with this, sitting down once again with smiles all around.

"Friends," said the pastor, "I want you to know that you have just touched one of God's masterpieces. You have touched a magnificent work of art, still on the easel, still in progress. The very handiwork of God Himself."

You and I could never be ordinary works of art. There is nothing "ordinary" about us. Because God is our artist, we are His masterpieces in process.

Unlike the curators of the Louvre, however, God treats His masterpieces quite differently. He invites us to draw near to each other, not to keep our distance. He encourages us to touch and embrace each other, to hug and to hold. Though each one of us is far more valuable than any painting ever created by human hands, we are not to be separated and segregated away from one another. In fact, our task as believers is more about removing the barriers between God's masterpieces. We have the unspeakable privilege of approaching God together and working side by side to advance His kingdom.

GOING DEEPER . . .

Let's see how inventive we can be in encouraging love and helping out, not avoiding worshiping together as some do but spurring each other on, especially as we see the big Day approaching.

HEBREWS 10:24-25, MSG

Keep on loving one another as brothers and sisters. Do not forget to show hospitality to strangers, for by so doing some people have shown hospitality to angels without knowing it.

HEBREWS 13:1-2

In God's great plan, we are privileged to help each other become the masterpieces of grace He intended. God wants you to draw near to others, perhaps even getting involved in repairing damage or mending hearts. He calls you to embrace, encourage, touch, and lift up the hearts of weary, discouraged souls around you, or those who are dealing with illness or injury. They may need a timely reminder that they are the handiwork of God in process—an eternal and deeply loved treasure.

- DAY 20 -

Future Joy

After so many years of dealing with affliction, I have come to the settled conviction that my heavenly Father values my faith more than any other quality of my life but love (see 1 Corinthians 13:2). In the great cosmic scheme of things, my faith is a very, very big deal to God.

As a result (I've finally figured this out), He sends me frequent troubles in order to try my faith. If my faith is worth anything, it will stand the test. Impurities are afraid of the fire, but gold is not. Gems made out of paste dread pressure, but a real precious stone can endure it. A fake Rembrandt will be quickly exposed, but an authentic masterpiece can pass the keen scrutiny of a professional art critic. When it comes to our faith, it doesn't say much when we can only trust God in the bloom of full health. True faith clings to the Lord even when the body is sick or disabled, and when spirits are depressed.

God absolutely delights in this kind of faith . . . faith that says with Job, "Though he slay me, yet will I trust Him" (Job 13:15, NKJV). This is faith that believes even when the smile of God is hidden from view.

The fact is, present afflictions and trials tend to heighten our future joy. A friend of mine recently told me about driving with his wife into a dangerous ice storm in the Pacific Northwest, with trucks jackknifing and cars sliding sideways. As the ice began to coat their windshield, turning their wipers into useless frozen clubs, they tried calling several hotels on their cell phone, but every one was booked up. When they finally found refuge at a nondescript motel a few miles away, it felt like arriving at a magnificent resort. Everything about that modest inn and its restaurant seemed utterly delightful. It was a warm, safe refuge from the danger, difficulty, and storm.

Peace when times are peaceful doesn't mean as much. But moments of peace in the midst of an upsetting, ongoing conflict become especially precious. The idea of rest can seem a little bit boring. But when that rest comes after a long, winding path up the side of a mountain with a pack on your back, it feels like pure paradise. Even sitting on a wide, flat rock can feel luxurious.

I'm convinced that the recollections of past sufferings may one day enhance the bliss of heaven. Eternity with the Lord will be so much more heavenly to those of us who have been tested, battered, and tried time and again. Remember that today in whatever difficulties you may encounter. God wants to strengthen your faith . . . and prepare you for joy.

GOING DEEPER . . .

But He knows the way that I take;
When He has tested me, I shall come forth as gold.

JOB 23:10, NKJV

In all this you greatly rejoice, though now for a
little while you may have had to suffer grief in
all kinds of trials. These have come so that the
proven genuineness of your faith—of greater
worth than gold, which perishes even though
refined by fire—may result in praise, glory
and honor when Jesus Christ is revealed.

I PETER 1:6-7

If the Lord highly values your faith, it makes sense that He will seek to test it, exercise it, and strengthen it. And when you respond in childlike trust in the midst of your difficulties and heartaches, it moves the heart of God. As your faith grows strong, so will your confidence of future joy with Him.

Eager Anticipation

My husband's friend Jan has two much-loved yellow Labrador retrievers named Star and Babe. And there is nothing in this world those two dogs love better than going bird hunting with Jan and Ken.

Show them a lake and they'll take a diving leap. Throw them a Frisbee and they will turn themselves into a knot to catch it. Let a bird cross their paths and they're ears-up and at 'em. These dogs are serious retrievers.

Not long ago Jan invited Ken on yet another

bird-hunting excursion. As soon as Babe and Star saw the Jeep loaded up with camping gear, they went ballistic. It was all Jan could do to restrain them. They were the very picture of eager, wildly joyous anticipation. They knew they were going, knew where they were going, knew what they were about to do, and couldn't wait for it to begin. All the way up the freeway and out into the high desert toward the pheasant farm, Babe and Star whined in their kennel. And when Jan turned down the road toward the farm, the dogs literally began rattling the cage, fully aware of the boundless pleasure that lay just ahead.

When God created Labrador retrievers, I think He must have been smiling. He gave us those beautiful, intelligent, willing, and happy dogs to remind us of what eager longing really looks like. Once Star and Babe realized where they were heading, they were overcome with anticipation, willing their master behind the wheel of the Jeep to drive faster!

In Philippians 3:20, the apostle Paul wrote, "But our citizenship is in heaven. And we eagerly await a Savior from there, the Lord Jesus Christ." *Eagerly*. I love that adverb. The dictionary defines it as "marked by enthusiastic or impatient desire or interest." Paul tells us that this sort of eagerness ought to mark our anticipation of the Lord's return and our future home in heaven. In other words, we ought to be rattling the cage and straining at the leash.

I have a bit of that eagerness myself. After long decades in this wheelchair with arms and legs and hands and feet that don't work, I'm more than ready to trade in this old body for a brand-new one. Better still, I'm ready to trade in my heart for a new one—and I can't wait for that day when sin and sorrow, sighing and suffering will be forever behind me. Just like Star and Babe, the joyful golden Labs, I know where I am going. And I can't wait to get there. This isn't a death wish—not at all. It's a life wish.

Let yourself get excited today as you think about the Lord Jesus coming in the clouds for you, giving you a new body in the twinkling of an eye, and taking you home with Him for all eternity.

GOING DEEPER . . .

Father, I want those you gave me
To be with me, right where I am,
So they can see my glory.

JOHN 17:24, MSG

For the Lord himself will come down from heaven,
with a loud command, with the voice of the
archangel and with the trumpet call of God, and
the dead in Christ will rise first. After that, we
who are still alive and are left will be caught up
together with them in the clouds to meet the Lord
in the air. And so we will be with the Lord forever.
Therefore encourage one another with these words.

I THESSALONIANS 4:16-18

Heaven really is THAT wondrous and Jesus truly is THAT awesome. Just five minutes with Him in the home He has prepared for you will be worth every tear on earth you ever cried. There's no shame in showing your eagerness to get there!

— DAY 22 —
The Slowness of God

METHUSELAH, a California bristlecone pine tree, is coming up on its 4,846th birthday. Squat, twisted, weathered, and storm-battered, it stretches jagged fingers toward the blue skies over the White Mountains in eastern California. It is alive and growing, although very, very s-l-o-w-l-y. It was already ancient when Jesus was born in Bethlehem, and it may very well last until He returns.

Looking at a picture of this amazing tree made me think of a passage I once read in a book by Frederick

Faber, an English hymn writer and theologian who lived a couple of centuries ago. "In the spiritual life," wrote Faber, "[God] vouchsafes to try our patience first of all by His slowness. . . . He is slow: we are swift and precipitate. It is because we are but for a time, and He has been from eternity. Thus grace for the most part acts slowly. . . . He works by little and by little, and sweetly and strongly He compasses His ends, but with a slowness which tries our faith, because it is so great a mystery. . . . We must wait for God, long, meekly, in the wind and wet, in the thunder and the lightning, in the cold and the dark. Wait, and He will come."

Yes, from our perspective God's grace sometimes moves slowly. Paul remained in a Caesarean jail for two long years before he finally arrived in Rome. God's people waited in Egypt four hundred years before they were ready for the next challenge. The Israelites sometimes camped in one spot in the wilderness for a year at a time, waiting for the cloud of God's presence to signal a resumption of their march to the Promised Land.

These thoughts comfort me as I ponder my

forty-seventh anniversary in this wheelchair. In that time, I have often had to wait for God in the wind and the wet, the heat and the dust, the cold and the dark. I've waited through tears, sighing, and long bouts of pain.

But do you know what? He does come. He always comes. He answers my call, meets my needs, and He is always right on time.

Does it seem to you that God's pace for your life has slowed down to a crawl? You may be waiting for healing . . . waiting for relief from your pain . . . waiting for a job . . . waiting for a mate . . . waiting for word from a wandering child. You must remember that "the Lord is not slow in keeping his promise, as some understand slowness" (2 Peter 3:9).

The important thing is to walk with Him, whether that pace seems slow or suddenly speeds up, as it often does. In Galatians 5:25, the apostle Paul had the best advice of all: "Keep in step with the Spirit."

The best thing in all of life is simply staying close to Him.

GOING DEEPER . . .

Don't be impatient. Wait for the Lord, and he
will come and save you! Be brave, stouthearted,
and courageous. Yes, wait and he will help you.

PSALM 27:14, TLB

In the morning, LORD, you hear my voice;
in the morning I lay my requests before you
and wait expectantly.

PSALM 5:3

You and I have one matchless, incomparable
advantage as we wait for the Lord to rescue us,
help us, or change our situation. He waits with us!
As He promised in Hebrews 13:5, "Never will I
leave you; never will I forsake you."

— DAY 23 —
Glow in the Dark

SOMETIMES, when you find yourself by an ocean at twilight watching the waves roll in, you might catch a greenish glow in the curl of a wave. Depending on the time of evening, the tide, and ocean currents, you may see a luminescence in the water: the glow of tiny creatures called plankton.

You may have never thought much about plankton, humble, microscopic organisms inhabiting our oceans. Yes, they're simple creatures, way down there on the food chain, but here is something you can admire: They glow in the dark. After absorbing sunlight all day on their aquatic journeys, they release an iridescent greenish-bluish light into the night. I remember camping in the summertime by the Delaware shore as a child and watching the soft glow on the undersides of the waves as they hurried to the shore.

Plankton have the quality of bioluminescence, which literally means "life that glows."

Jesus calls on us as His followers to have that same essential quality. He wants us to glow in the dark. Yes, Jesus is "the light of the world," but in Matthew 5:14-16 He turned that around and said to us, "You are the light of the world . . . a town built on a hill . . . a lamp . . . on its stand."

It's a life that glows, even in the dark. Perhaps especially in the dark. The apostle Paul urged us to be "'children of God without fault in a warped and crooked generation.' Then you will shine among them like stars in the sky as you hold firmly to the word of life" (Philippians 2:15-16).

Through the years, Ken and I have been in some very, very dark places in this world as we have sought to bring help and hope to disabled people in forgotten, impoverished cities and villages. The darkness can be both literal, an absence of electricity and streetlights, and spiritual, where Satan and his hordes hold a tightfisted grip over so many broken lives. But we have met radiant believers in such places, men, women, and children whose lives shine in the darkness, clear and clean as starlight.

Are you in a dark place today? Your darkness today might involve illness, depression, physical pain, financial troubles, marriage struggles, or worry over loved ones on a dangerous path. But the more time you spend in the presence and conscious awareness of Jesus Christ—reading His Word, speaking to Him, and earnestly cultivating His presence—the more your life will take on His glow. You will be noticed in spite of yourself, and draw attention . . . to Him.

GOING DEEPER . . .

*Nothing between us and God, our faces shining
with the brightness of his face. And so we are
transfigured much like the Messiah, our lives
gradually becoming brighter and more beautiful
as God enters our lives and we become like him.*

2 CORINTHIANS 3:18, MSG

*Those who are wise will shine like the brightness
of the heavens, and those who lead many to
righteousness, like the stars for ever and ever.*

DANIEL 12:3-4

Even when you don't have the time or opportunity to speak a word for Christ, you can still do this: You can spend time in His presence, soaking up His light, and then allow that light to shine in whatever dark or uncertain situation you find yourself.

Arise, Shine. . . .

EVEN THOUGH I am not a morning person, I have learned over the years that it is the most important time in my day.

When the alarm goes off my head is groggy, my thoughts are foggy, and I have zero inclination to bound out of bed into a new day (even if I could—which I can't). Desperately craving another hour of sleep, I lie there thinking about someone coming into my bedroom to give me a bed bath, give me range-of-motion exercises, do toileting routines, get me dressed, sit me up in my wheelchair, push me to the bathroom, brush my teeth, blow my nose, brush my hair, and . . . I tell the Lord, I don't have energy for this. I can't do this. That is my natural, unvarnished, human response to another day as a quadriplegic.

When I was a child, before my injury, it wasn't that way. I would hear my mother call from downstairs, "Rise and shine!" She sounded so upbeat and cheery, no wonder I threw back the covers to race downstairs for breakfast. But I don't race anywhere now, and my quadriplegia seems more of a challenge to me than it ever has before.

That's why I cling to Isaiah 60, verse 1. It's a verse for my mornings, and maybe it will become the verse for your mornings too: "Arise, shine, for your light has come, and the glory of the LORD rises upon you." My friend Lynn, who struggles with mornings as I do, told me, "As I meditate on this Scripture, it occurs to me that the glory of the Lord is upon me, whether I feel it or not. It rises with me on each new day."

I am making it my goal to step into that reality. If

the glory of the Lord rises upon me with every fresh, new morning, I want to agree with God. I want to rise and invite the light of the Lord Jesus to illumine my day. The Bible assures me that "my light has come" (see Isaiah 60:1), so I tell my soul to come into alignment with the Word of God. As my girlfriends get me dressed and sit me up in my wheelchair, I tell my heart to listen to the Scripture and answer the call of God on my life.

My friend, I encourage you to do the same. Time and again, as you look back on your life, God truly has met you with the dawning of each new day. His mercies are new every morning, the Bible says, and He graciously pours out those mercies upon you.

You have every reason to rise and shine.

GOING DEEPER . . .

Wake up, sleeper,
rise from the dead,
and Christ will shine on you.

EPHESIANS 5:14

As I think you have realised, the present
time is of the highest importance—it is
time to wake up to reality. Every day brings
God's salvation nearer. The night is nearly
over; the day has almost dawned. . . . Let
us arm ourselves for the fight of the day!

ROMANS 13:11-12, PH

Morning is a time to celebrate God's faithfulness and His fresh mercies on your life for the day ahead. What kind of change to your morning routine might help you meditate on these truths and bask in His presence as the sun rises?

— DAY 25 —
Somebody Is Watching

As MUCH AS WE may try to deny it, we behave differently when we know for sure we're being observed. We bite our tongues, hold our tempers, or restrain our impulses. We make more of an effort to be pleasant and helpful. This is why Hebrews 12:1 is at once so convicting and so encouraging:

> Therefore, since we are surrounded by such
> a great cloud of witnesses, let us throw off

everything that hinders and the sin that so easily entangles. And let us run with perseverance the race marked out for us.

I know the Lord is always watching (and yes, that ought to be motivation enough), but it still makes a difference when I consider that my earthly father—now in heaven—may also be observing me. When I'm tempted to blurt out malicious remarks or do something I'd be embarrassed about if I were found out, I stop, reminding myself that I'm surrounded by witnesses. A host of Old and New Testament saints, as well as departed family members and Christian friends (I think of Corrie ten Boom), are watching me, cheering me on toward obedience, faithfulness, and perseverance. Somehow, this thought helps inoculate me against the temptation of foolish, private sins. Scripture also seems to indicate that God's holy angels observe our lives and consider our ways (see Hebrews 13:1-2; 1 Peter 1:12; 1 Corinthians 11:10).

When you're driving by yourself, how do you respond when someone cuts you off in traffic? What do you do in a hotel room with an array of cable channels at your fingertips? Perhaps nothing deters us better from hidden, so-called "secret" sins than the knowledge that others—perhaps hundreds or thousands—are observing us, willing us to win the battle and stay faithful to Christ.

I believe the cosmic stakes and eternal ramifications of each day of our lives are incredibly high, far beyond what we might imagine. For now, earth is a battleground between vast spiritual forces, and we have only one brief lifetime to prove our faith and our love for Christ.

When Jacob woke up from his dream of a heavenly staircase, with God Himself at the top and His angels coming and going, he was filled with awe. He said, "Surely the LORD is in this place, and I was not aware of it. . . . How awesome is this place! This is none other than the house of God; this is the gate of heaven" (Genesis 28:16-17).

That's the sort of awe we should have about the place we are right now. In reality, everywhere we go and every-place we rest is "the gate of heaven" . . . if only we had eyes to see.

GOING DEEPER . . .

Whatever happens, conduct yourselves in a manner
worthy of the gospel of Christ. Then, whether I come
and see you or only hear about you in my absence,
I will know that you stand firm in the one Spirit,
striving together as one for the faith of the gospel.

PHILIPPIANS 1:27

Take time today to imagine faces in the celestial grandstands who—right now—may be observing your obedience, your faith, your mind-set, and your perseverance. Stop periodically to acknowledge God's presence—"How awesome is this place!"

— DAY 26 —
Ride Death Close

I WAS RAISED on a farm with three older sisters who loved horseback riding. Every weekend they would saddle up and race down the trail. I may have only been four or five years old, but I admired the fearlessness in my older siblings, and I didn't want to be left in the dust.

With those thoughts in mind, my first horse was no benign little pony; it was a sixteen-hand-high Appaloosa mare named Thunder.

The very first time I sat atop Thunder, she bolted and

I slid off the saddle. I remember protesting loudly when Daddy tried to set me on her back again. When Thunder saw the fear in my eyes, she tossed her head and shied away. The horse obviously had the upper hand.

"You must get back up on her, Joni," my dad said. "If you don't, Thunder will know you are afraid of her, and she'll never obey you!" After thinking for a moment or two about my sisters and their courage, I yielded to my father. He placed me atop my horse and stepped back. Mimicking my sisters, I slapped the reins and gave a hearty click with my tongue. I wanted my unruly horse to know I was in charge. And I was. The big mare obeyed my signal and trotted forward. From then on, we were friends. I will never forget my dad's words of affirmation: "That 'a girl, Joni! Now you're riding her close!"

Facing death as a believer is much the same. If we cower before its shadow, the next time it approaches will seem even more terrifying. And although dying is a fearful subject, when we face up to it, we break its power over us, like breaking a horse. Yes, death is still much larger and stronger than us, but fears of death need not control us. When we engage, examine, and talk about it—when we ride death close—we can say, "Even though I walk through the valley of the shadow of death, I will fear no evil, for you are with me; your rod and your staff, they comfort me" (Psalm 23:4, ESV).

The apostle Paul, who faced death again and again before his eventual execution in a Roman dungeon, described a believer's passing as being "swallowed up by life" (2 Corinthians 5:4). In other words, when the moment finally arrived, it wasn't death that took him at all . . . it was Life with a capital *L*.

GOING DEEPER . . .

*As long as I'm alive in this body, there is good work
for me to do. If I had to choose right now, I hardly
know which I'd choose. Hard choice! The desire to
break camp here and be with Christ is powerful.
Some days I can think of nothing better. But most
days, because of what you are going through, I am
sure that it's better for me to stick it out here. So I
plan to be around awhile, companion to you as your
growth and joy in this life of trusting God continues.*

PHILIPPIANS 1:22-25, MSG

Lord, thank You for the magnificent homecoming You have planned for me in the very instant I step out of this life. In the meantime, help me to make the very most of this day of life on earth, pointing as many people as I can toward the path of Life.

Weaving Straw into Gold

PSALM 138:8 SAYS, "The LORD will fulfill his purpose for me" (ESV).

Now there is a verse of Scripture that has buoyed my spirits in difficult times. In her classic devotional book *Streams in the Desert*, Mrs. L. B. Cowman wrote,

There is a divine mystery in suffering, one that has a strange and supernatural power and has never been completely understood by human reason. For no

one has ever developed deep spirituality or holiness without experiencing a great deal of suffering. When a person who suffers reaches a point where he can be calm and carefree, inwardly smiling at his own afflictions, and no longer asking God to be delivered from it, then the suffering has accomplished its blessed ministry. . . . At that point, the pain of the crucifixion has begun to weave itself into a crown.

Oh, the contentment of being able to smile at your own afflictions! I am so very glad that those anxious, fretful days of "Man, I am sick and tired of this stupid wheelchair" are far behind me. Now when I lie in bed at night and look at my empty wheelchair over in the corner of the bedroom, I smile. I recognize what it has accomplished in my life over nearly five decades.

How about the things that crucified you in the past, those events, circumstances, or disappointments that bruised you, pulled you down, or even crushed you? Are those experiences now being woven into a crown? As we wait with patience for the Lord to strengthen and sustain us, we really do begin to feel the weight of our cross being exchanged for the weight of a crown. Nothing can match the glorious assurance that your pain has been transformed. It's difficult to put the outcome into words. You experience a fresh stillness before the Lord. Contentment comes so much more easily. Complaining becomes a thing of the past, as you no longer fantasize about castles in the clouds or pie in the sky. And the only choice that really matters is choosing Jesus in all things, letting circumstances be what they may. That is contentment so sweet and secure that I wouldn't trade it for anything. Not even a whole body.

Do you have the calm assurance that God truly is causing all things—good and bad, past and present—to "work together for good," as it says in Romans 8:28 (ESV)?

May your cross soon become your crown.

GOING DEEPER . . .

My heart is not proud, LORD,

my eyes are not haughty;

I do not concern myself with great matters

or things too wonderful for me.

But I have calmed and quieted myself,

I am like a weaned child with its mother;

like a weaned child I am content.

PSALM 131:1-2

For our present troubles are small and won't last very long. Yet they produce for us a glory that vastly outweighs them and will last forever! So we don't look at the troubles we can see now; rather, we fix our gaze on things that cannot be seen. For the things we see now will soon be gone, but the things we cannot see will last forever.

2 CORINTHIANS 4:17-18, NLT

In the old fairy tale, Rumpelstiltskin took straw and wove it into gold. May our loving God, for whom nothing is impossible, transform your hurts and hardships into outcomes that are sweet beyond words.

— DAY 28 —
Not Why but How

I LEARNED to stop asking God why a long time ago. But I frequently ask Him how. How can I go forward? How can I endure this? How can I stay positive and productive as I battle chronic pain?

The fact is, I receive letters from people who struggle with pain far, far more than I do. And frankly, I don't know how they do it. A woman named Barbara has been bedridden for over ten years, and there are only two positions she can get into, neither of which is comfortable.

Barbara's pain is off the charts, and her sleep comes only in little bits. When she reached out to me, I felt so helpless. What could I say to her? How could I help her?

The key is right there in the word *how*. Don't ask God why, but rather ask Him how. How do we keep on? How do we live? How can we care about others when we carry such a heavy load ourselves? How can we be kind and civil when we are racked with pain so much of the time?

My friend Dr. Michael Easley, who suffers constant pain from degenerative disk disease, will often say, "Just do the next thing." It's what I tell myself when pain intrudes, elbowing and clawing its way into my day. I will say, "Joni, just do the next thing." It's overwhelming at times, and I tire of the journey, but God remains faithful and kind to us in the midst of our suffering.

We live in a terribly fallen world. Remembering this, I comfort myself knowing that while I am a sinner deserving only hell and punishment, He has by His grace and kindness saved me eternally, and this life is only temporary. My pain—and Barbara's, and yours—is just a tiny little taste of the hell from which Christ has rescued us.

So, friend, if you are dealing with pain today, or depression or grief or paralyzing anxiety, I encourage you to "just do the next thing." It may mean simply getting out of bed or up off the couch. Or getting out of the house. Or doing the laundry or washing those dishes that have been sitting in the sink. And as you do it, ask Him to give you joy in some small but noticeable way.

Press on as best you can, and lean into His embrace. And take heart. One of these days you will hear those wonderful words from your Savior, "Well done, good and faithful servant," all because you got up and did the next thing.

GOING DEEPER . . .

*Dear brothers and sisters, when troubles come
your way, consider it an opportunity for great joy.
For you know that when your faith is tested, your
endurance has a chance to grow. . . . If you need
wisdom, ask our generous God, and he will give
it to you. He will not rebuke you for asking.*

JAMES 1:2-3,5, NLT

What is the "next thing" in your life today? Ask
the Lord for the grace and courage to step into it,
whatever it is.

The Lord Bless You. . . .

THE OTHER DAY an old friend stopped by my office for a visit. As he was leaving, he turned at the doorway and said, "God bless you, Joni."

Immediately I replied, "And I receive it!"

We didn't say those words to be polite, cordial, or pleasant. We both meant it. I want to keep my heart open and receptive to any blessings or favor from God that might be coming my way, and I want to announce that intention to any angel or demon who might be listening in.

What's more, I want to make sure God Himself hears me say that I am open, receptive, and happy to receive whatever life, divine energy, or supernatural joy He desires to impart to me. Many times, I have found, He gives me that kind of grace and energy when a Christian brother or sister chooses to speak a blessing over me.

Yes, I know that the word *blessing* has become something of a Christian cliché. We will say, "Someone bless the food," rattle off a quick "Bless you" when we part from friends, or maybe sign off an e-mail with the term "Blessings." It's a nice way to speak, of course, but when we use that term so nonchalantly, we allow it to be drained of its actual significance and power. In reality, a blessing is serious business.

In the book of Numbers, the Lord was so intentional about this matter of blessing others that He gave His servant Moses precise instructions. He said, "This is how you are to bless the Israelites. Say to them: 'The LORD bless you and keep you; the LORD make his face shine on you and be gracious to you; the LORD turn his face toward you and give you peace'" (6:23-26). Then God added, "So they will put my name on the Israelites, and I will bless them" (verse 27).

In other words, this isn't just some easy, convenient phrase to toss out there like "So long" or "See you later"; this is (or should be) a divine transaction.

For however many days the Lord gives me on earth, I want to receive His blessings, and I want to give His blessings. The apostle Paul said that when God makes His face to shine upon you, He enables you to shine in that same way—to actually shine with the reflected glory of God (see 2 Corinthians 3:18).

The more you absorb the Lord's presence throughout your day, the more you will have to shine out to others. They will catch a glimpse of Jesus Himself in your smile, and in your eyes.

GOING DEEPER . . .

So all of us who have had that veil removed can see
and reflect the glory of the Lord. And the Lord—
who is the Spirit—makes us more and more like
him as we are changed into his glorious image.

2 CORINTHIANS 3:18, NLT

Surely, LORD, you bless the righteous;
you surround them with your favor as with a shield.

PSALM 5:12

Today—this very day of your life—is all about receiving and giving. First, receive the favor, love, kindness, and light God has for you in Christ, but then release it to others at the first opportunity.

Stop the Inner Churning

WE KNEW there would be traffic. After all, this was LA. But who would have imagined this much traffic, inching along like a sleepy glacier? The extra time cushion we had given ourselves to get to my important crosstown appointment melted away. With ten minutes to go, we were stuck on the highway more than ten miles out . . . which might as well have been one hundred miles. As the minutes ticked by I felt tension, frustration, and yes, I was becoming angry.

It was with an effort that I remembered God Himself was in control of that morning traffic, and if He had me in that situation, it was for His reasons and His purposes. There was something for me to see and learn in that irritating circumstance. Mostly, He wanted me to trust Him, seek Him, and rest in Him, rather than mentally cursing the unknown drivers causing the slowdown.

Anger reveals much about our hearts and motives. Maybe it's pride over what others might think of us, or greed, demanding of life that all the trees lean our way. Anger reveals what's really going on inside—and it may not be pretty. Irritating situations like traffic jams, broken washing machines, missed appointments, and even fender benders don't just flow in and out of our lives without reason. Every irritating problem is allowed and purposed by God to force you and me to examine our hearts, confess wrong responses, and ultimately draw closer to the Lord.

Psalm 46:1 tells us that "God is our refuge and strength, an ever-present help in trouble." The psalm goes on to describe all sorts of amazing confusion, dislocation, noise, and desolation—including kingdoms falling and mountains plunging into the sea. But then it ends with these words: "Be still, and know that I am God; I will be exalted among the nations, I will be exalted in the earth" (verse 10). The literal translation for *be still* is "cease striving."

And that is wonderful advice. Be still . . . cease striving . . . stop the inner churning . . . and realize that you belong to a powerful, loving, infinitely wise God who ultimately controls all things. When you are in a frustrating situation that lies beyond your ability to change or solve, let go of the anger, confess the wrong attitudes your temper has revealed, and simply rest in Him.

GOING DEEPER . . .

God is a safe place to hide,
ready to help when we need him.
We stand fearless at the cliff-edge of doom,
courageous in seastorm and earthquake,
Before the rush and roar of oceans,
the tremors that shift mountains.

Step out of the traffic! Take a long,
loving look at me, your High God.

PSALM 46:1-3,10, MSG

If today you find yourself in an irritating circumstance, a frustrating situation, stop and examine your heart, then ask God's help in resolving that anger so you can draw closer to Him. It is the wise and peaceful thing to do.

Tears at the Pool

SOME TIME AGO, Ken and I had the chance to visit the Holy Land. Ken sketched out an itinerary for us, but since I didn't really look at it ahead of time, I didn't know what he had planned. But I was happy he had arranged for us to visit the Old City of Jerusalem. He bumpety-bumped me in my wheelchair down the steps of the Via Dolorosa, through the Arab Bazaar, past the Sheep Gate, made a left-hand turn by Saint Anne's Church, and then turned us down a cobblestone path.

Suddenly we came into an open area, and I knew right where we were. "Oh, my goodness, look at this! Oh, Ken—it's the pool of Bethesda! Oh, sweetheart, you wouldn't believe how many times I used to imagine myself here."

It was a dry, dusty afternoon, and the place was empty and quiet. Ken hopped the railing, running down into the cistern to see if there might be any water left in the pool. I leaned against the guardrail, imagining once again the many sick and disabled people lying there, waiting to get healed. Huge tears came pouring out of my eyes, because God was so precious to give me this moment with Himself in the place I had seen so often in my mind's eye.

"Thank You," I whispered. "Thank You for the healing You gave me. The deeper healing. Oh, God, You were so wise in not giving me a physical healing. Because that 'no' has meant 'yes' to a stronger faith in You, a deeper prayer life, and a greater understanding of Your Word. It has purged sin from my life, forced me to depend on Your grace, and increased my compassion for others who hurt. It has stretched my hope, given me a lively, buoyant trust in You, stirred an excitement about heaven, and pushed me to give thanks in times of sorrow. It has increased my faith and helped me to love You more. Jesus, I love You more."

He didn't give me the physical healing I had wanted, but the deeper healing I needed so much more.

Maybe your prayer has been, "God, why won't You remove my problem? Why won't You change my situation? Why won't You heal me—from this pain, this sickness, this struggle, this disability?"

The fact is, He might! He might remove that "thorn in your flesh," and sooner than you think. But in the meantime, He might also use that suffering to draw you closer to His heart, shaping and forming you for purposes beyond your imagination.

So let Him have His way in your life.

GOING DEEPER . . .

So then, those who suffer according to God's
will should commit themselves to their
faithful Creator and continue to do good.

I PETER 4:19

For it is God who is at work within you, giving
you the will and the power to achieve his purpose.

PHILIPPIANS 2:13, PH

The One who has the power to heal and make
changes in your life has long-term—even eternal—
purposes in mind. He will transform you, His
deeply loved child, from glory to glory. That is the
deeper healing, and you don't have to break your
neck to receive it!

INTERNATIONAL DISABILITY CENTER

If you wish to write to Joni or learn more about
the ministry of Joni and Friends, contact:

Joni and Friends
PO Box 3333
Agoura Hills, CA 91301

www.joniandfriends.org
818.707.5664